Manga Sisters

Saori
Takarai

Misato
Takarai

Manga Sisters

MANGA UNIVERSITY

Gift Books

TOKYO   SAN FRANCISCO

Manga Sisters
By Saori Takarai and Misato Takarai

Published by Manga University under the auspices of Japanime Co. Ltd.,
3-31-18 Nishi-Kawaguchi, Kawaguchi-shi, Saitama-ken 332-0021, Japan.

www.mangauniversity.com

Editor: Glenn Kardy
Project coordinator: Mari Oyama
Translator: Mieko Kurosawa
Editorial assistants: Jakub Makalowski and Dale Rubin

Special thanks to the Society for the Prevention of Cruelty to Manga Characters.

First edition, September 2007

ISBN-13: 978-4-921205-18-8
ISBN-10: 4-921205-18-3

10 9 8 7 6 5 4 3 2 1   y 15 14 13 12 11 10 09 08 07

Printed in China

To: _____

From: _____

Introduction

Saori and Misato Takarai know exactly what it means to be "manga sisters."

The two artists grew up near Tokyo and, like most siblings, learned how to be both competitive and cooperative as they dealt with parents, teachers, boyfriends and — perhaps most challenging of all — each other.

And when it became clear they had a knack for drawing cute pictures, they began using manga to express their innermost thoughts and feelings.

Now, as young adults, they have teamed up to offer this lighthearted look at the very special relationship shared by sisters everywhere.

Sisters share
a sense of discovery
that goes far beyond
the looking glass.

姉妹とは、日常生活の境界を超えた、
特別な感性を分かち合っているものだ。

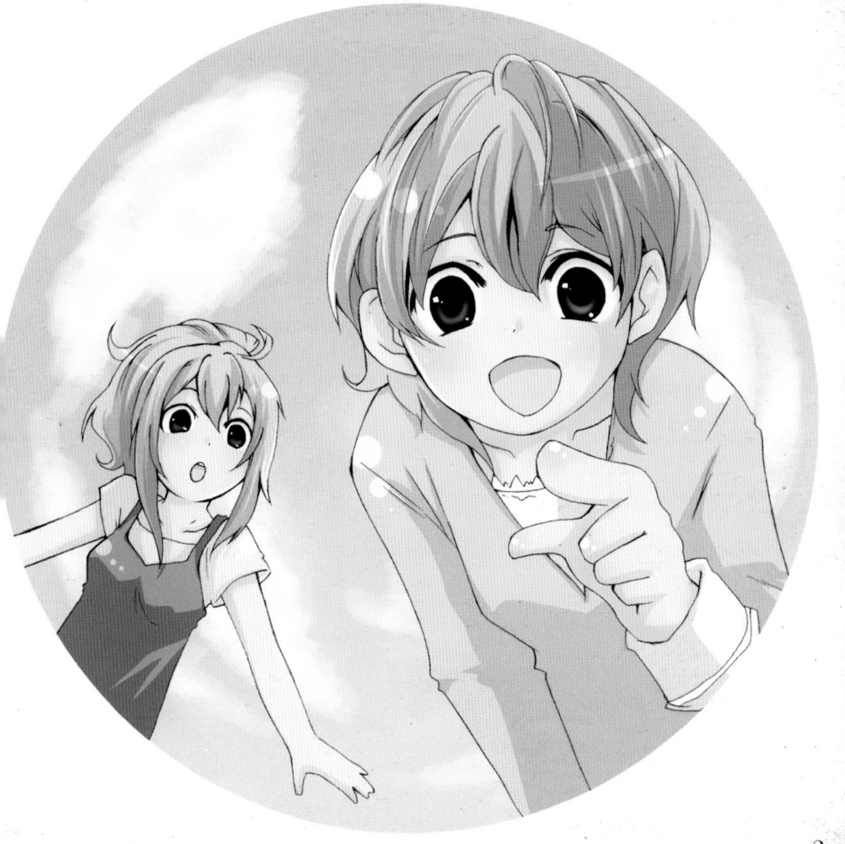

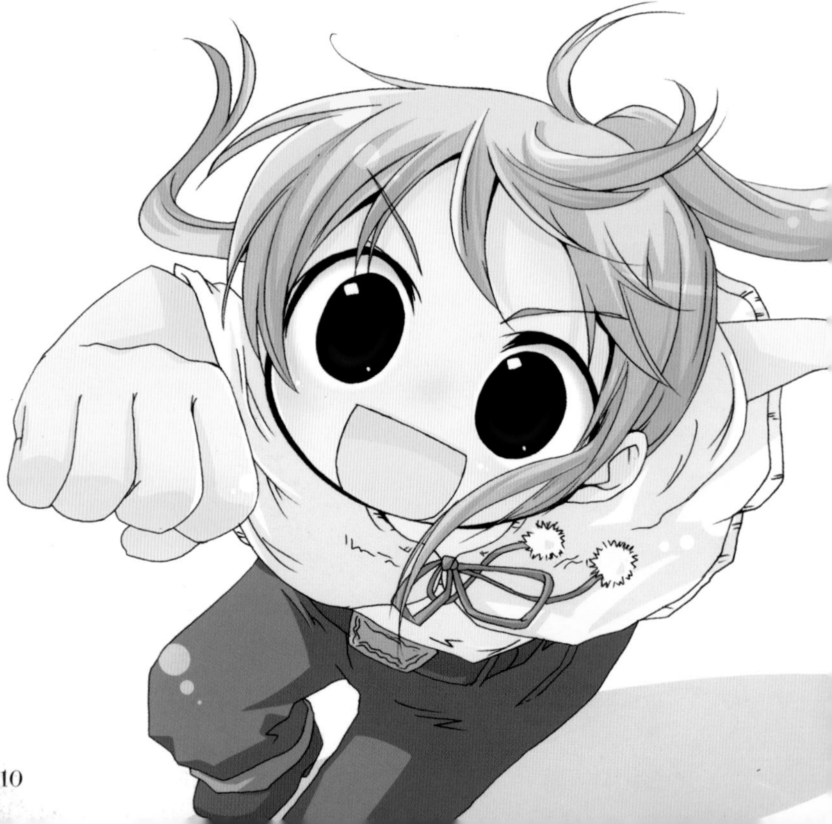

Big sisters
give new
meaning
to the phrase
"follow
the leader."

姉というものは
「指導者に従え」という言葉
に新しい意味を与える。

Sisters are
the very definition
of "teamwork."

姉妹というものは、「チームワーク」
という言葉そのものだ。

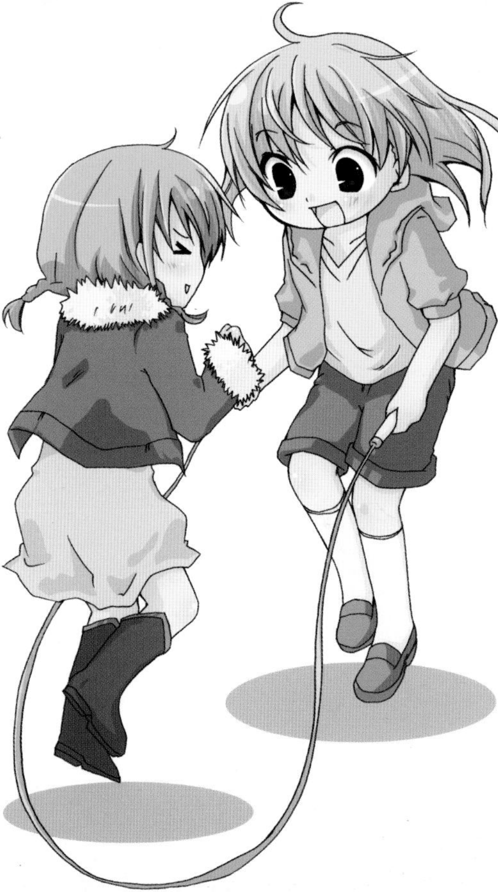

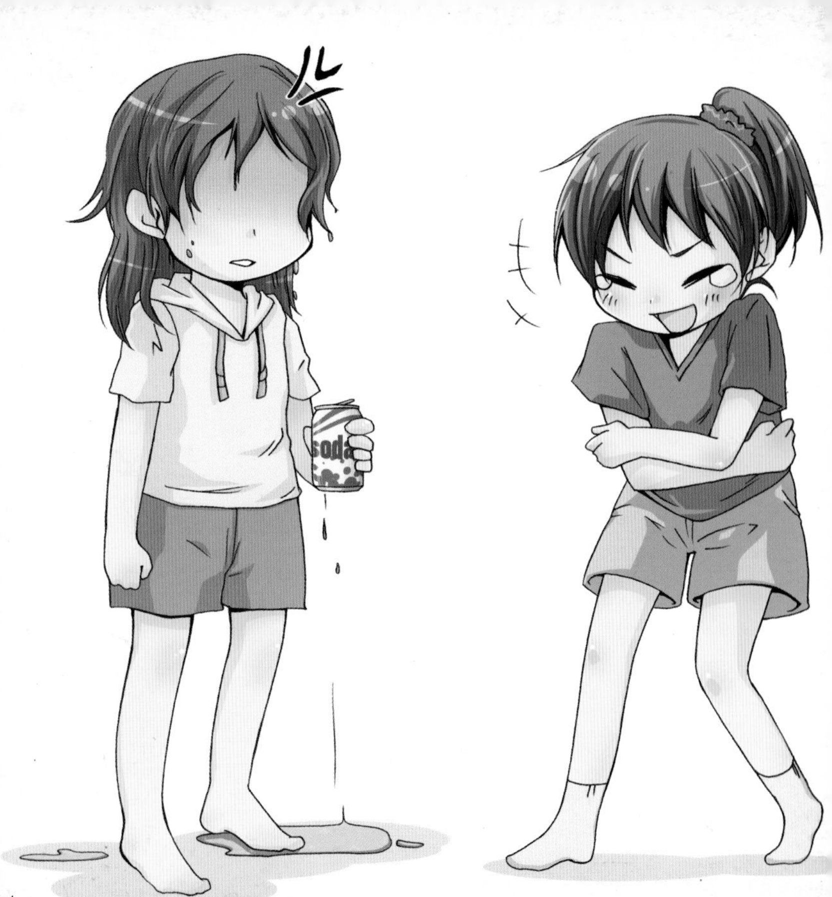
soda

It wouldn't be
so embarrassing
if your sister
wasn't there.

妹に見られていなかったら、
こんなに恥ずかしくないのに。

10 out of 10 sisters agree:

10人中10人の
姉妹とも、

Homework is a pain!

宿題は嫌！
という意見に賛成する。

Your sister
always makes
you feel like
a million bucks.

妹はいつもあなたを励まし、
力づけて自信を持たせてくれる。

18

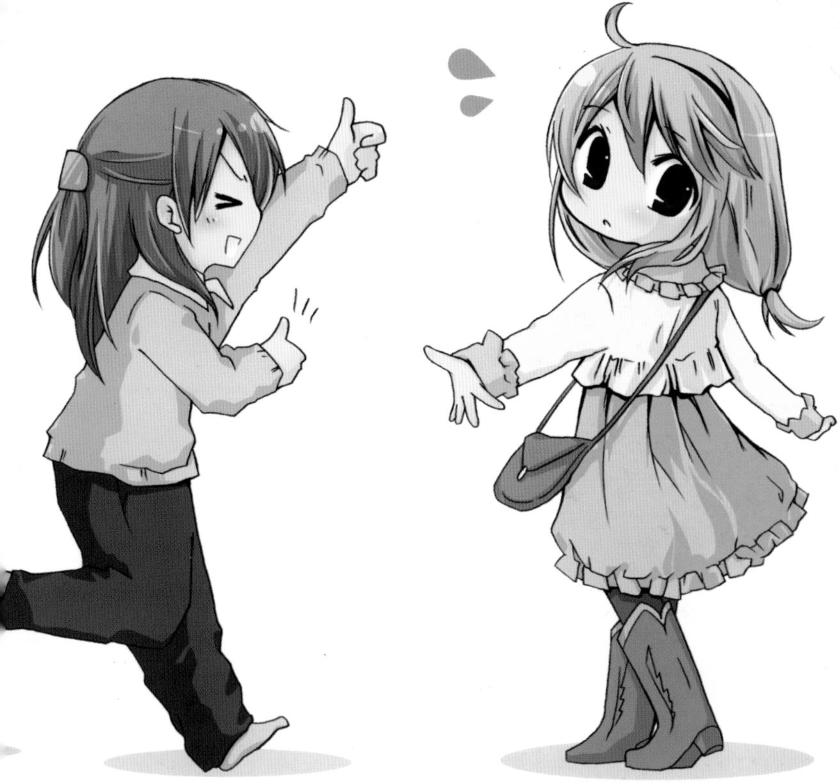

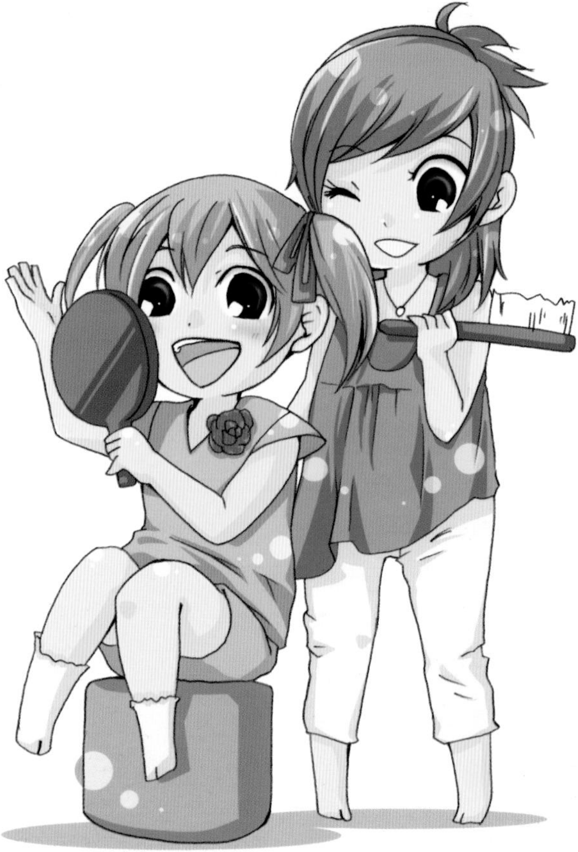

Who needs
a hairdresser
when you have
a big sister?

お姉さんさえいてくれれば、
美容院なんて行かなくてもいい。

RULE #1:
Never share cheat codes with your sister.

ルールその一：妹には 絶対に
ゲーム隠しコマンドを教えないこと。

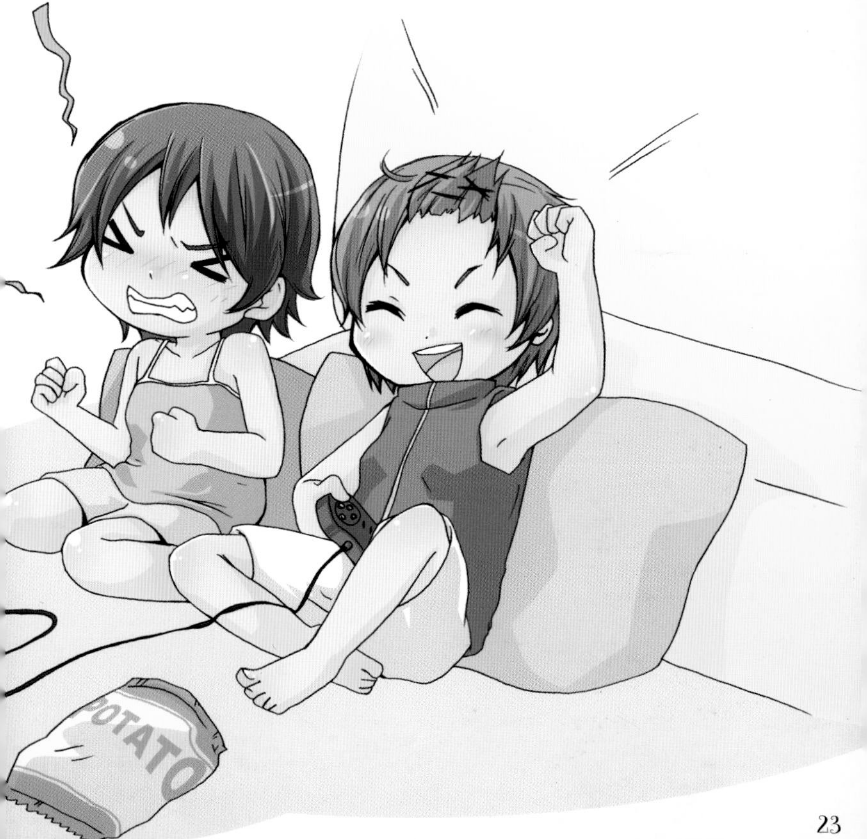
POTATO

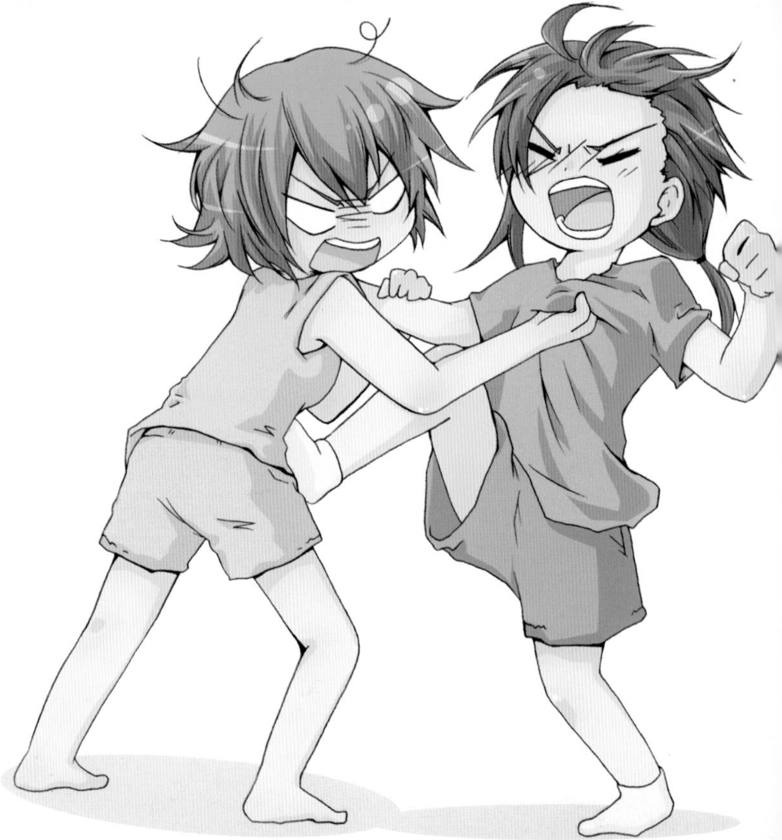

The phrase
"cat fight"
was undoubtedly
invented by
two sisters.

キャットファイトという言葉はまぎれもなく、
二人の姉妹が喧嘩をする様子を見て
生み出されたに違いない。

When the going gets tough, sisters go shopping!

何か嫌な事があったら、
姉妹は買い物に繰り出す！

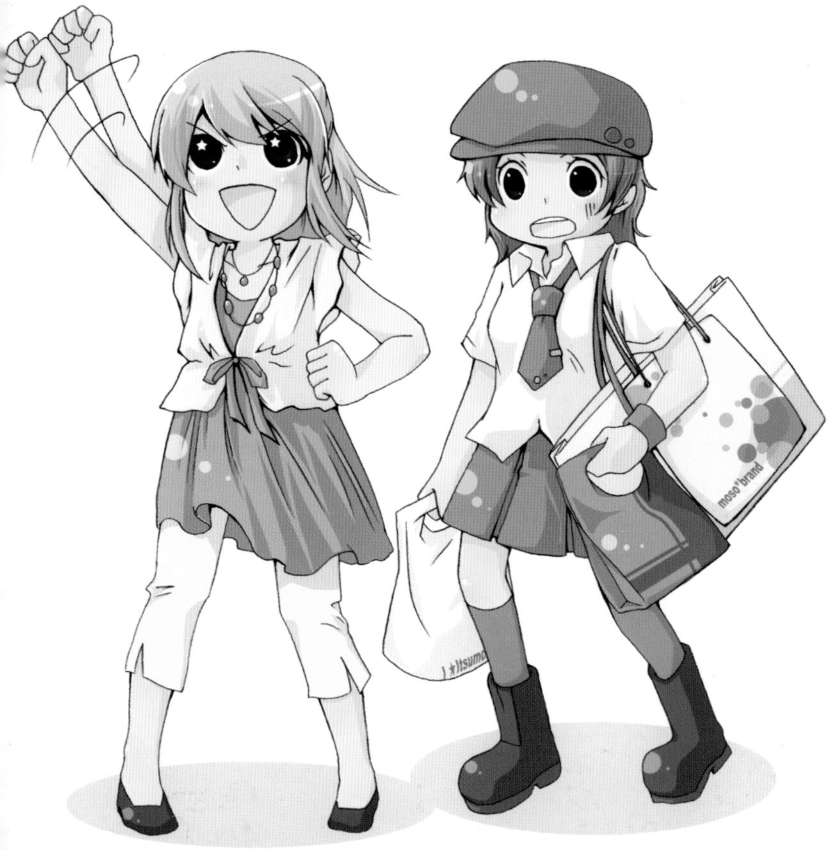
moso*brand

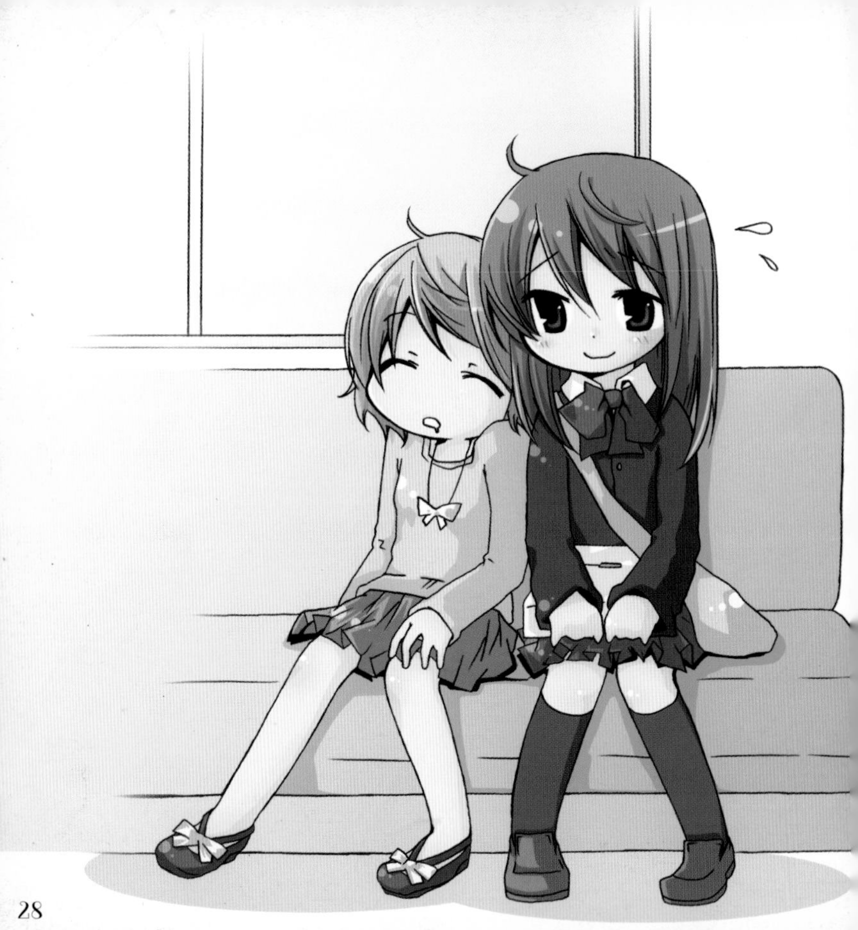

A sister's shoulder
is the world's most
comfortable pillow.

姉の肩というのは、
世界一快適な枕である。

You can borrow
her clothes,
jewelry
and money,
but never take
your sister's
ice cream.

姉の服、アクセサリー、お金は
借りてもいいが、アイスクリームに
だけは手を出さないこと。

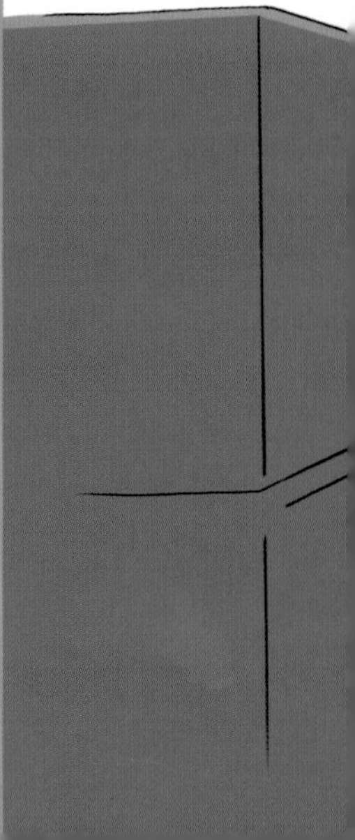

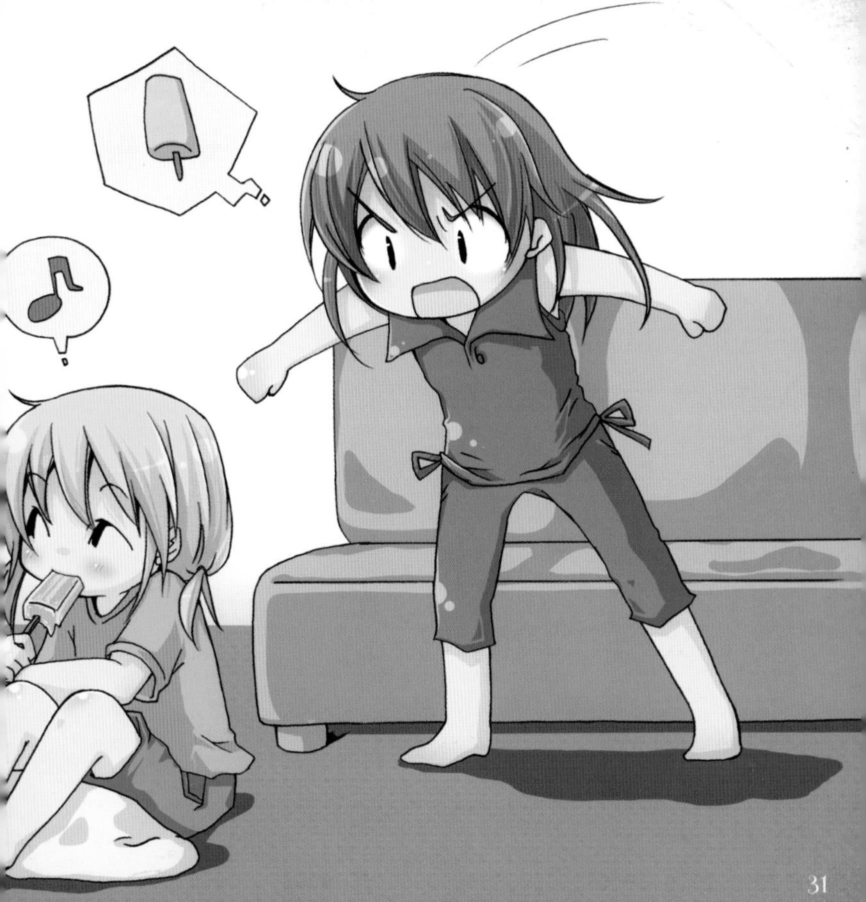

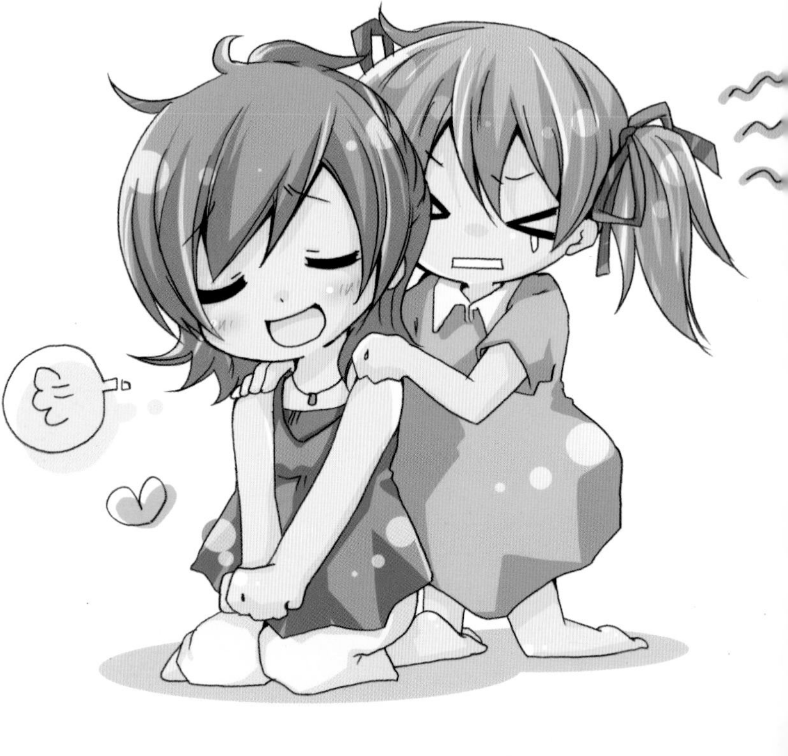

Back rubs
are a little sister's
labor of love.

肩をもむのは妹の姉に
対する愛の証。

Big sisters
always remember
your first case
of puppy love.

姉は妹の初恋を覚えているものだ。

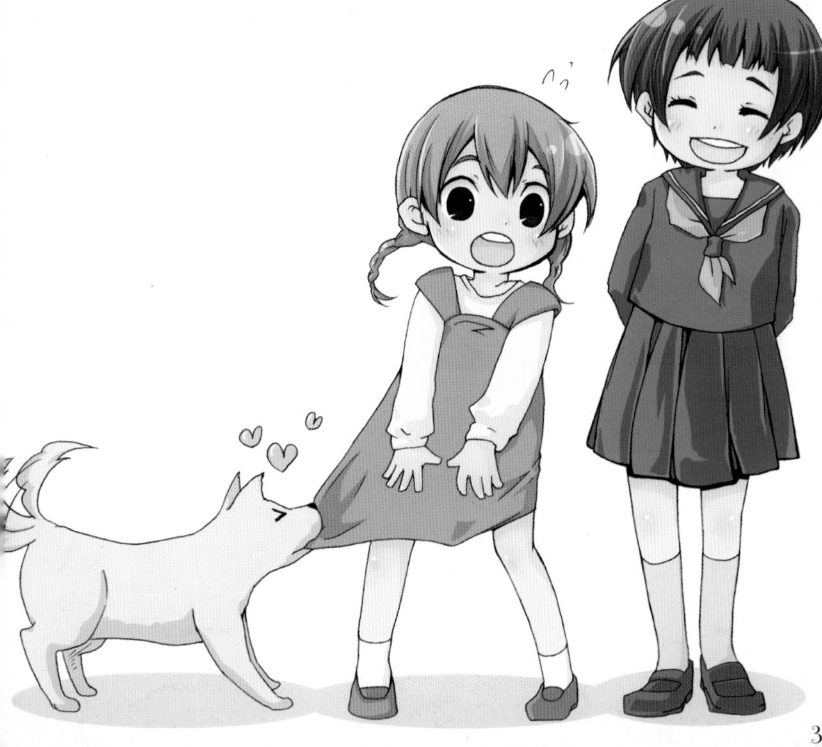

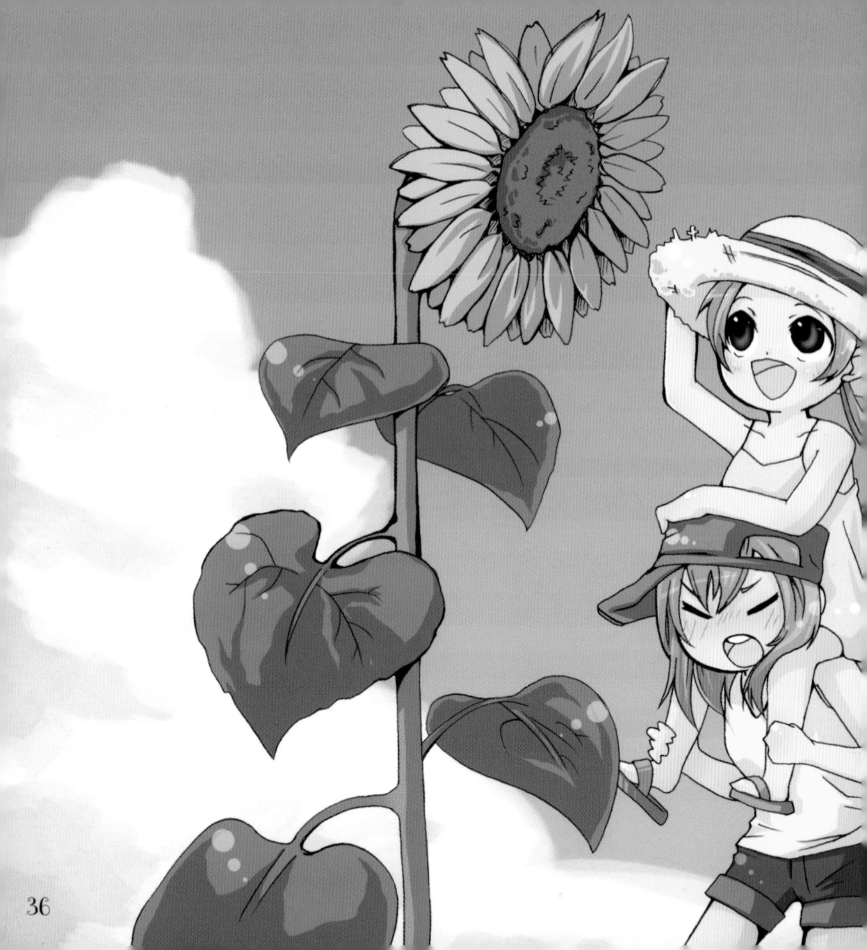

She ain't heavy, she's your sister.

重くない、重くない。
妹だもの。

Sisters
don't let sisters
apply makeup
without mirrors.

姉は妹が鏡を見ないで
化粧させない。

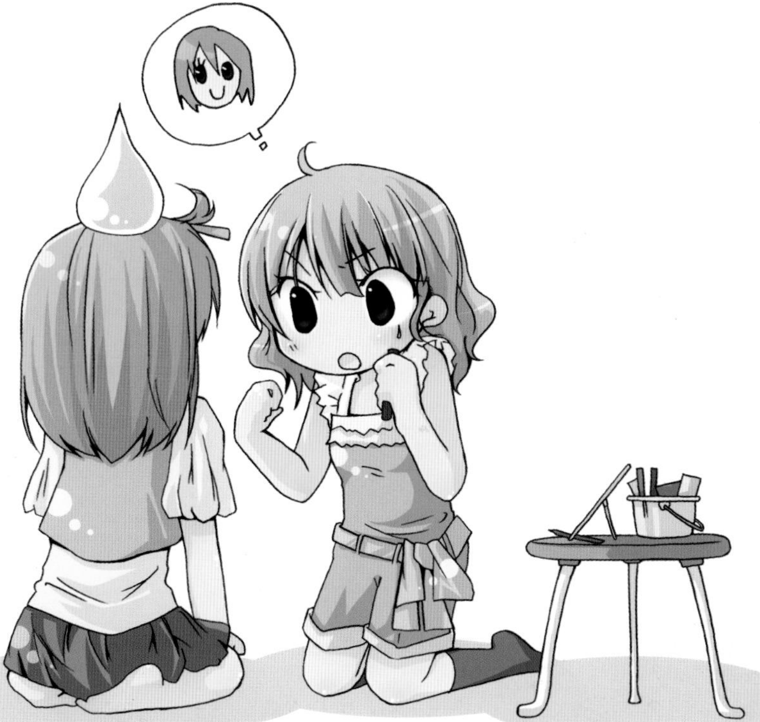

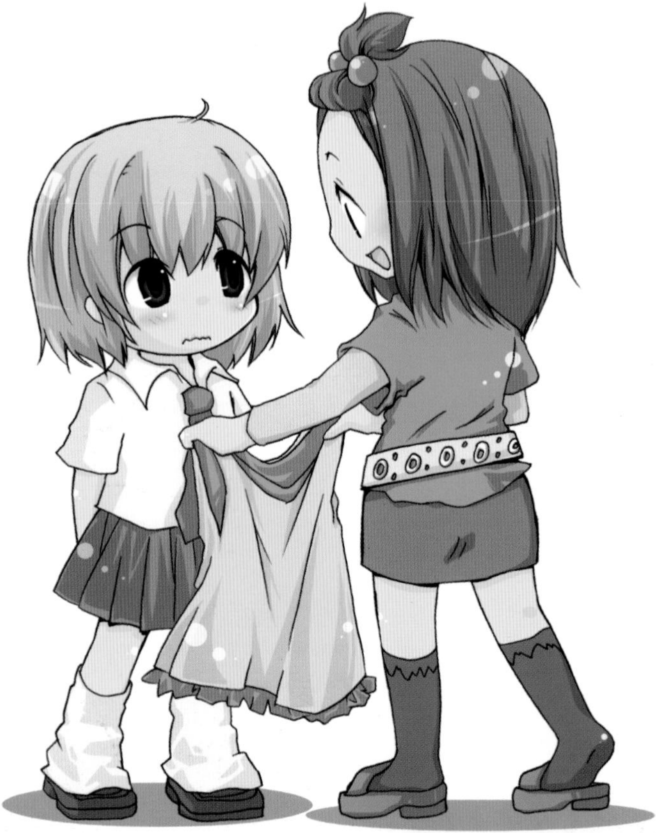

Hand-me-downs
are the worst part
about having
a big sister.

姉がいて一番損をすることは、
おさがりを着なくてはならないこと。

Your sister
can even make
folding clothes
kinda fun.

姉と一緒にやれば、
洗濯物をたたむのも楽しい。

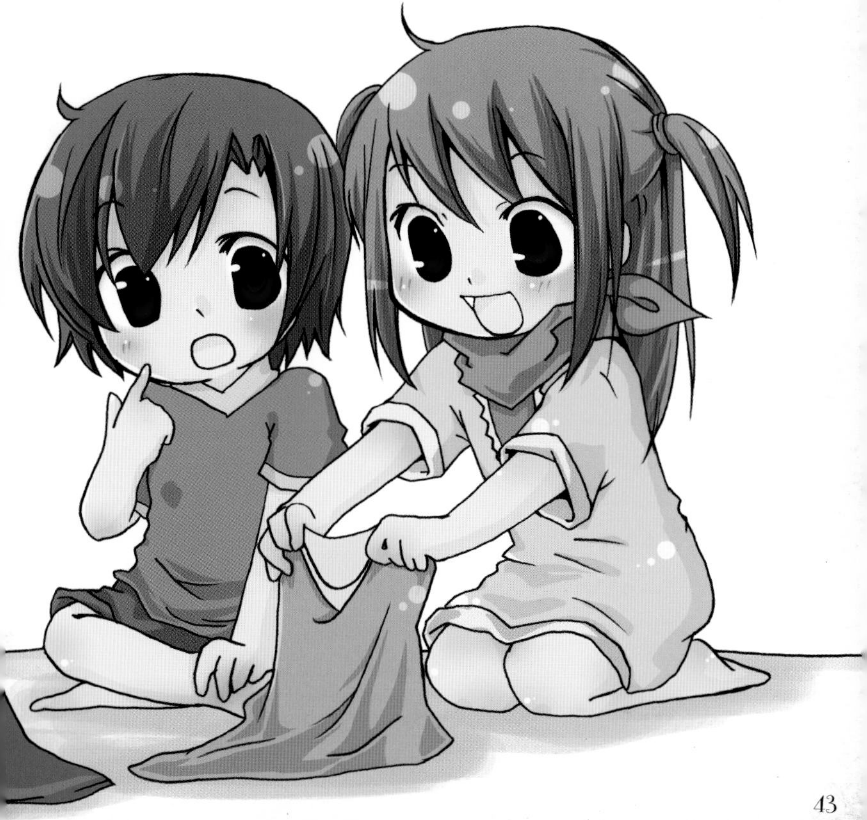

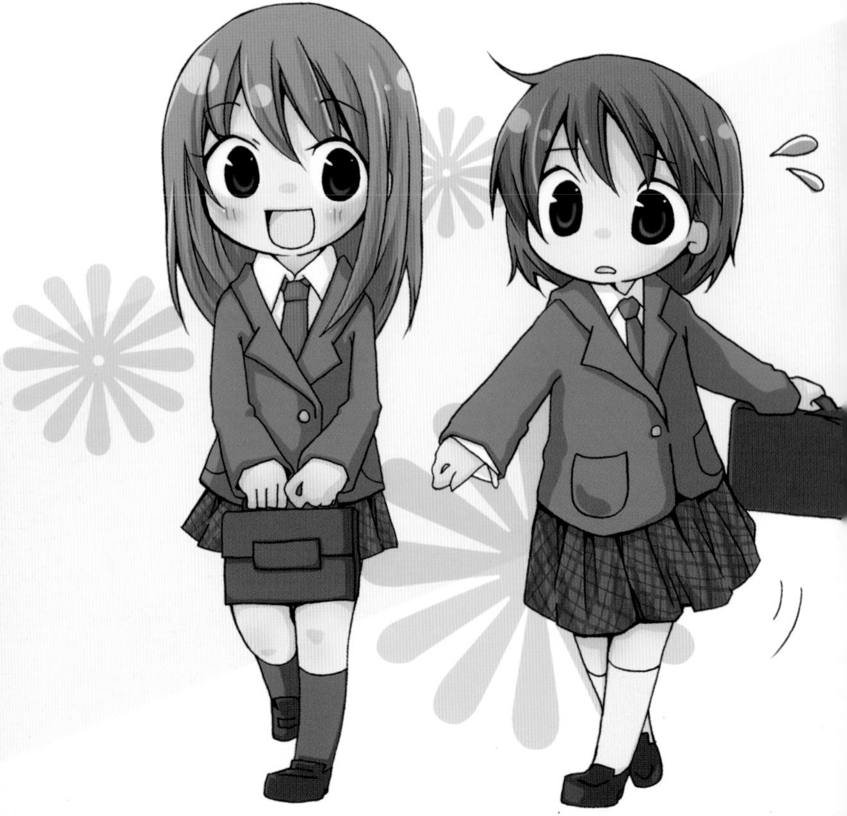

The first day of school
isn't so bad
when your sister
shows you the way.

学校の初日も、姉さんがいろいろ
教えてくれれば怖くない。

Sisters who let
a teddy bear
tear them apart...

テディベアの取り合いで
喧嘩した姉妹は…

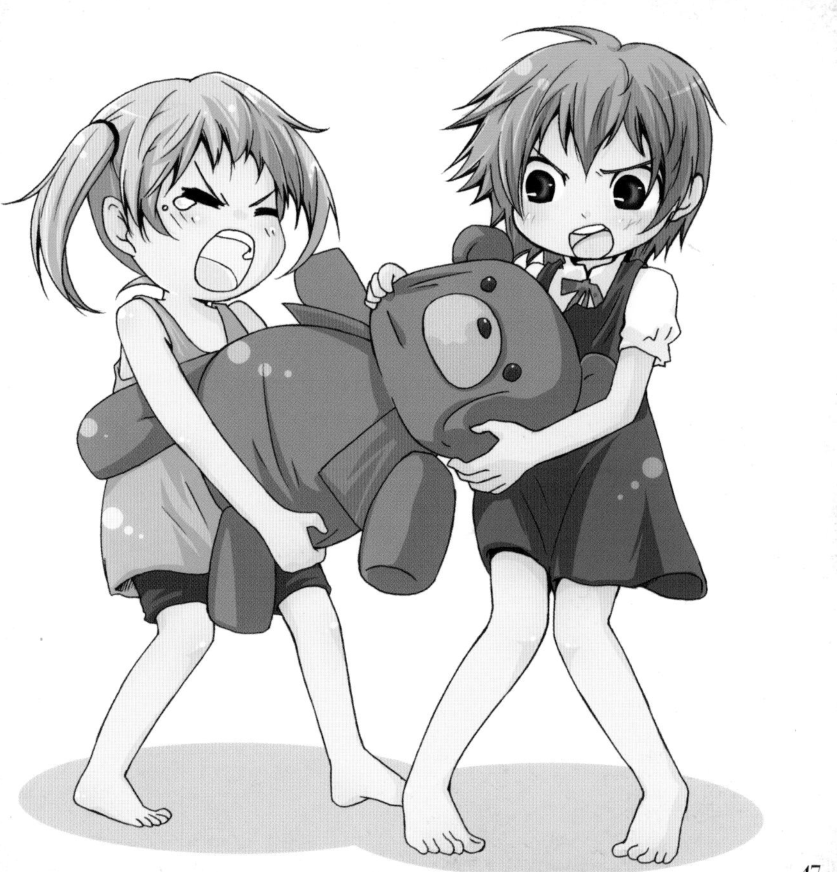

...will soon
learn their
lesson!

すぐに自分たちの行動の
結果を思い知ることになる！

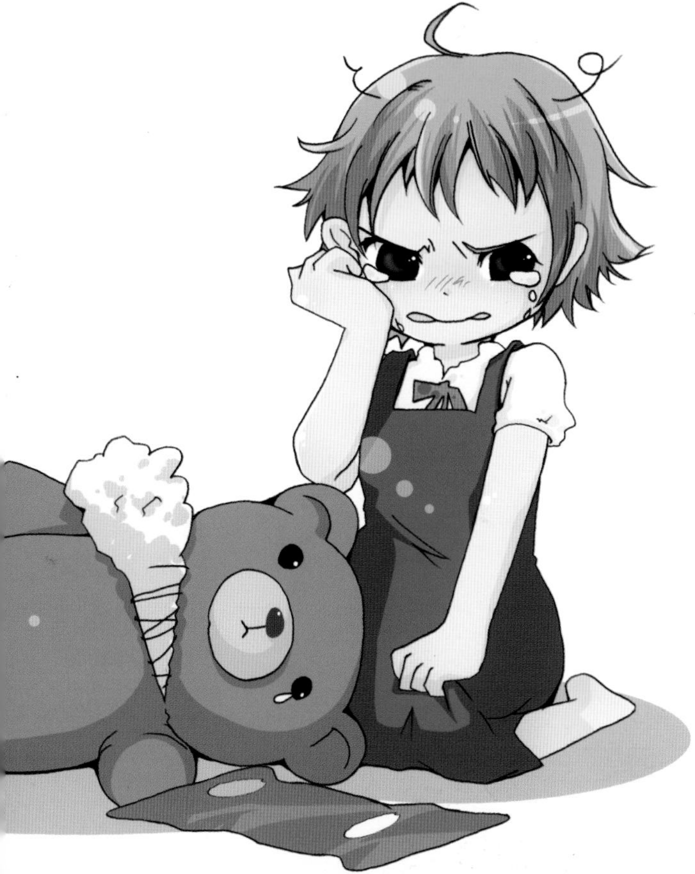

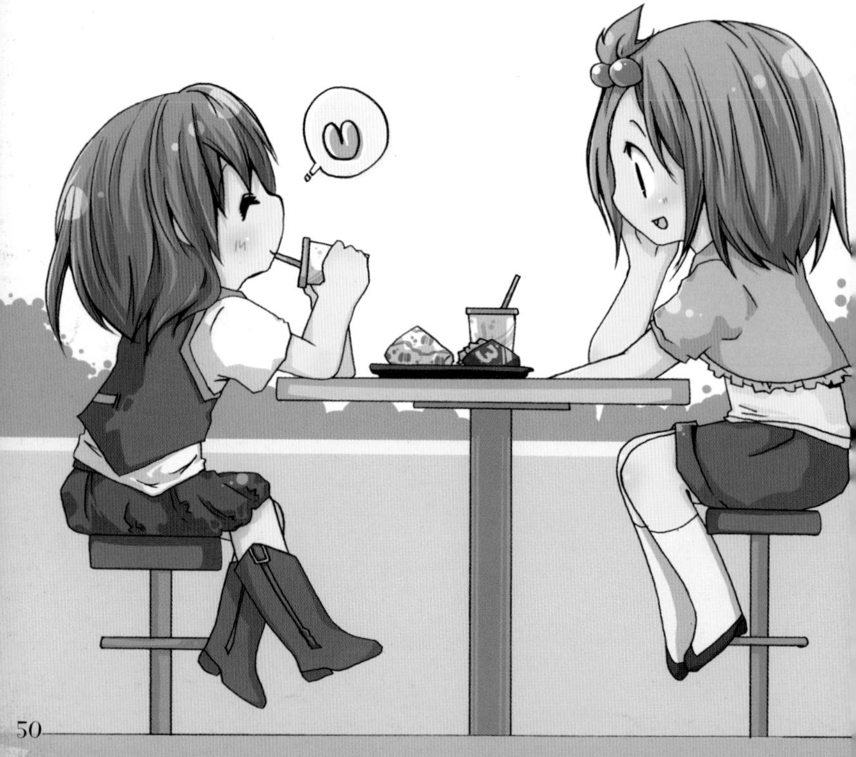

Hearing that
your sister is in love
is the next best thing
to being in love yourself.

妹が恋をしているのは、自分が
恋している次にいいものだ。

Just because
she's your big sister
doesn't mean
she's a good cook.

お姉さんだからといって料理が
得意とは限らない。

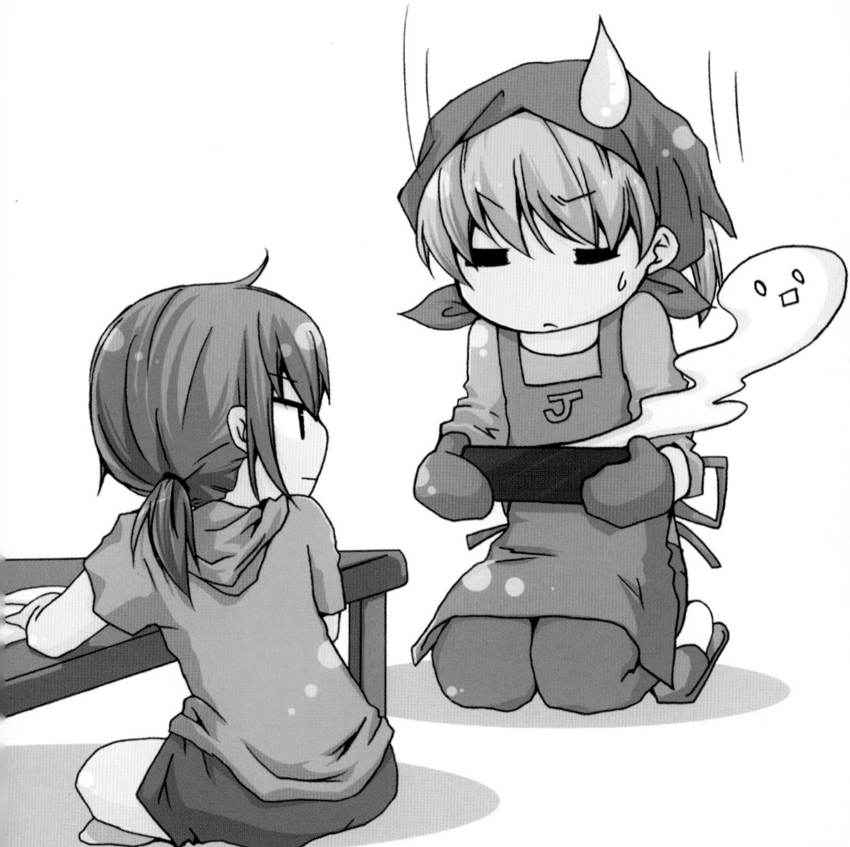

Sisters know when to share...

姉妹は二人で分け合う時を知っているけど・・・

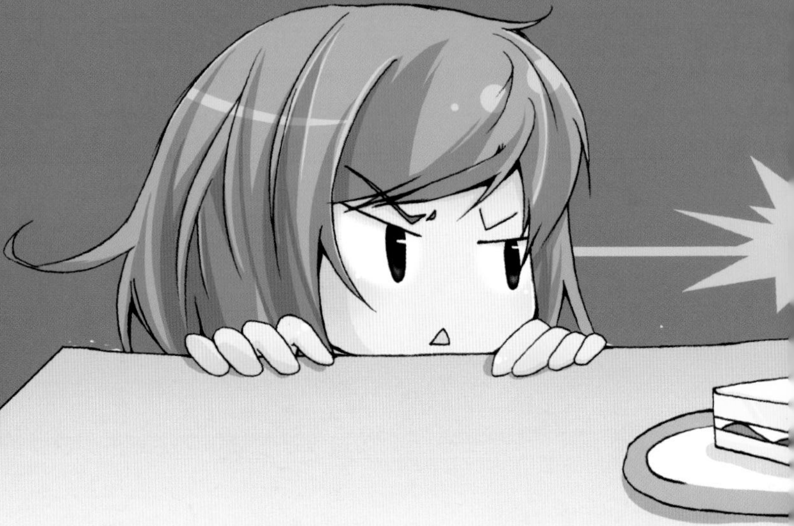

And right now's
not that time!

今はその時ではない！

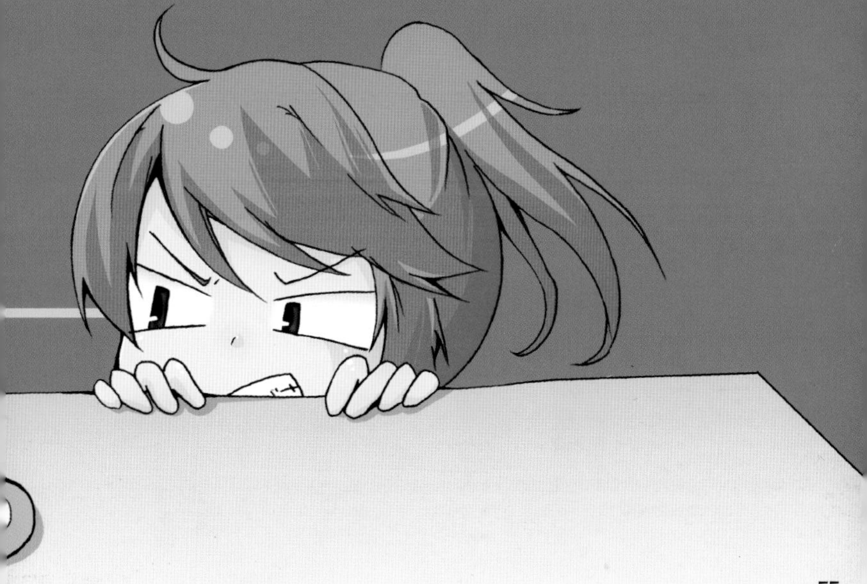

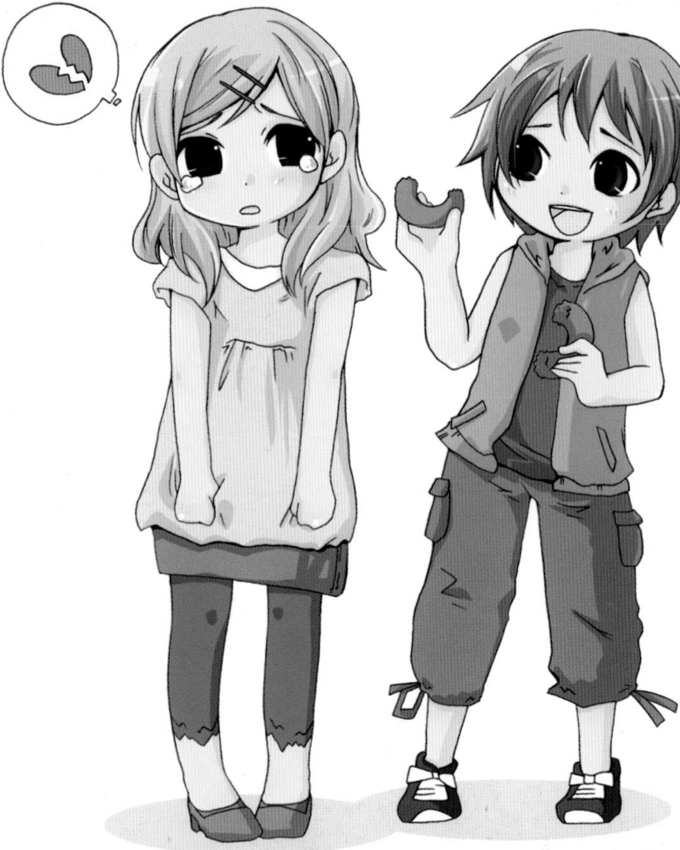

Your sister
always knows
how to mend
a broken heart.

姉はどうやって傷心の妹を
元気づければいいか知っている。

Next to moms,
big sisters
are the
best teachers.

母親の次に、姉は二番目に
優れた教師だ。

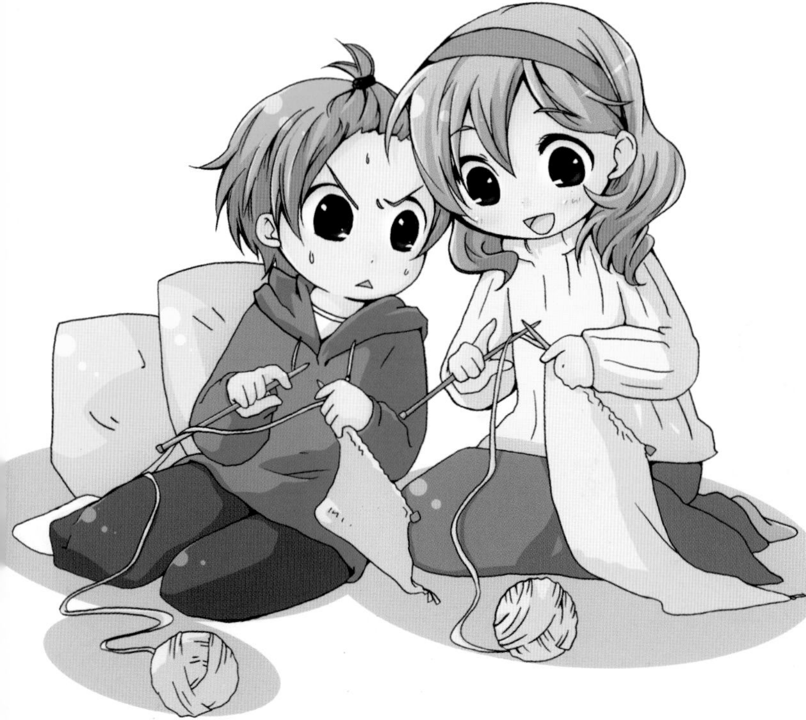

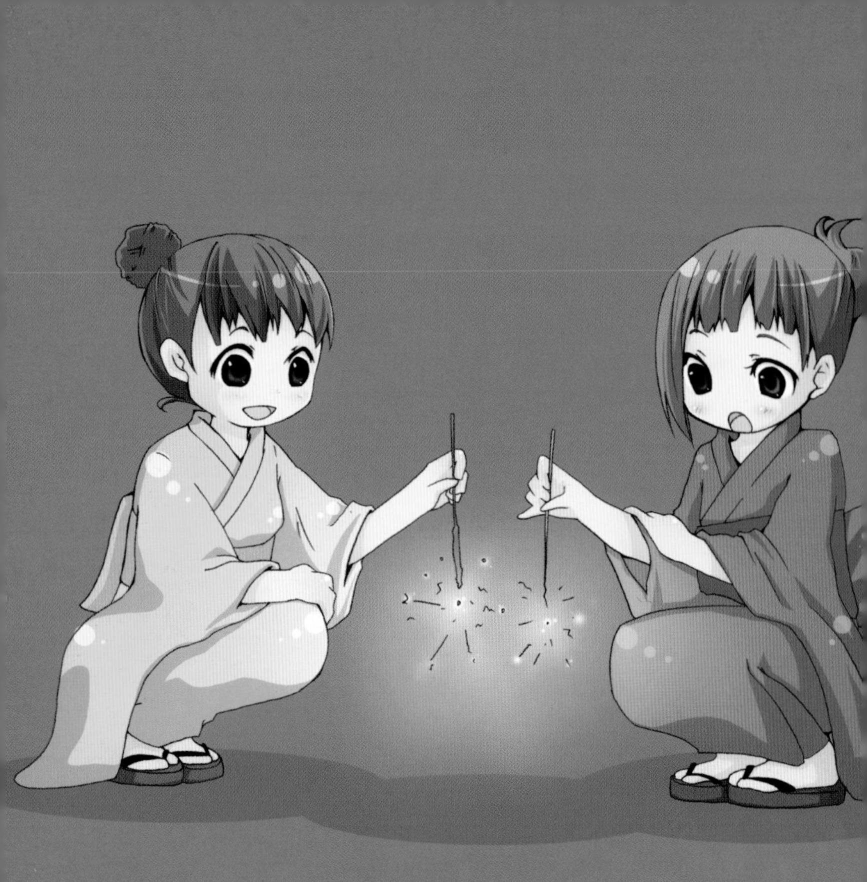

A sister's love
is the most
spectacular thing
you'll ever experience.

姉妹愛はあなたが体験するなかで
もっともすばらしいものだ。

Summertime
is sisters-time.

夏は姉妹の季節。

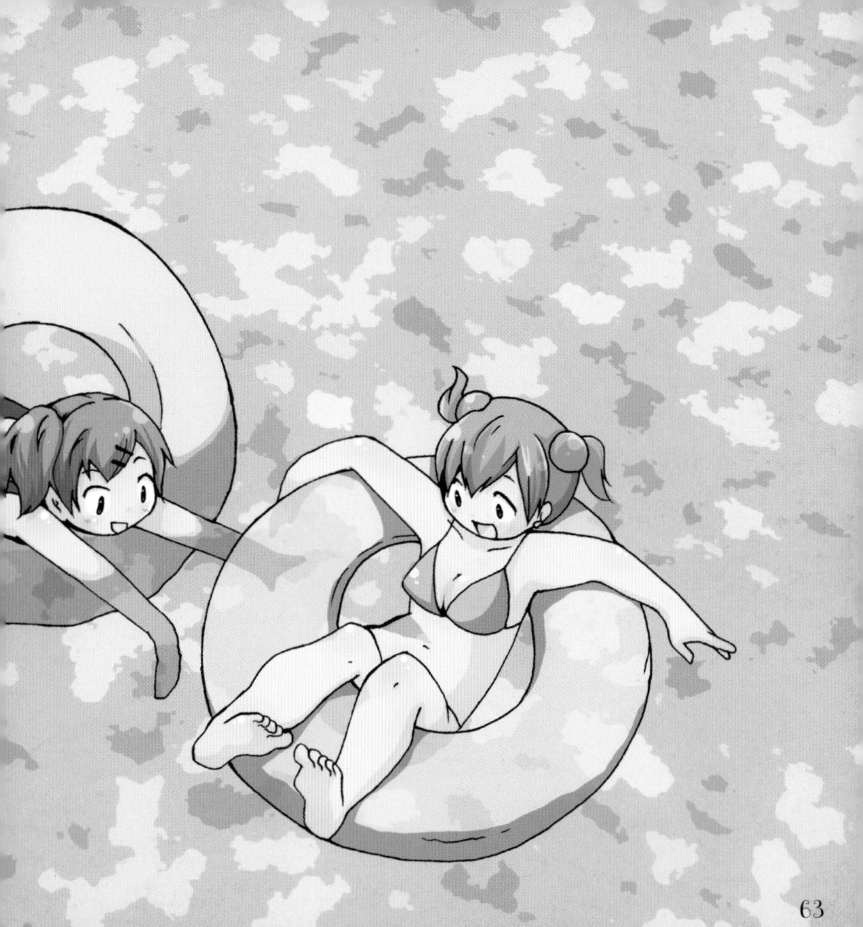

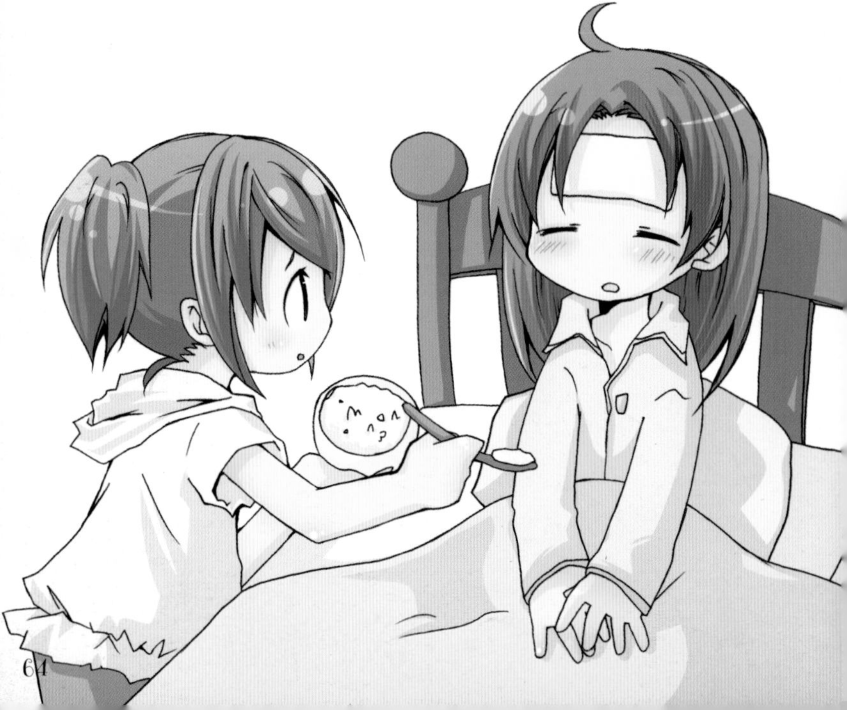

A sister's love
is the best cure
for whatever
ails you.

元気が無いときは妹の愛情が
一番の特効薬。

The easiest way
to upset your sister
is to fall in love
with a boy she likes!

姉を怒らせる一番の方法は、
同じ男の子を好きになること！

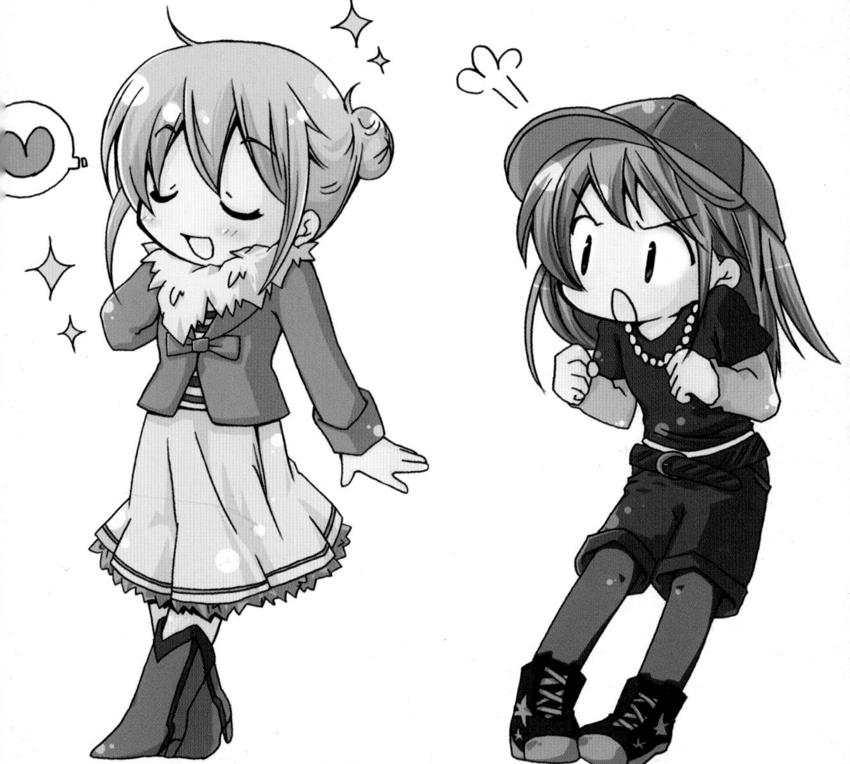

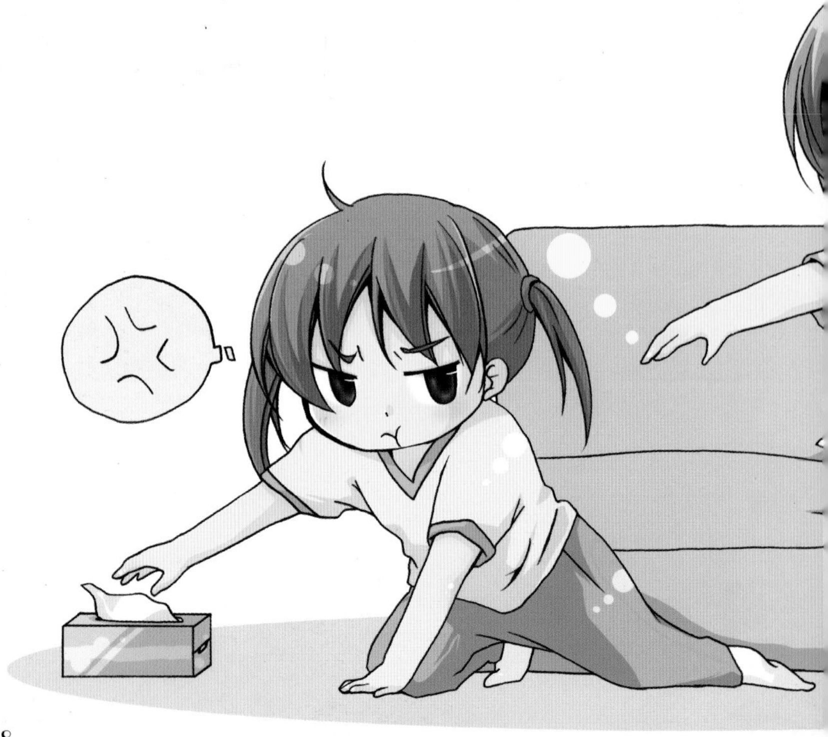

Always remember: She's your little sister, not your servant.

忘れないで：
妹であって、
召使いではないのですよ。

Alone time
is best spent
with your sister
at your side.

一人で静かに過ごすとき、
妹がそばにいるのは楽しいものだ。

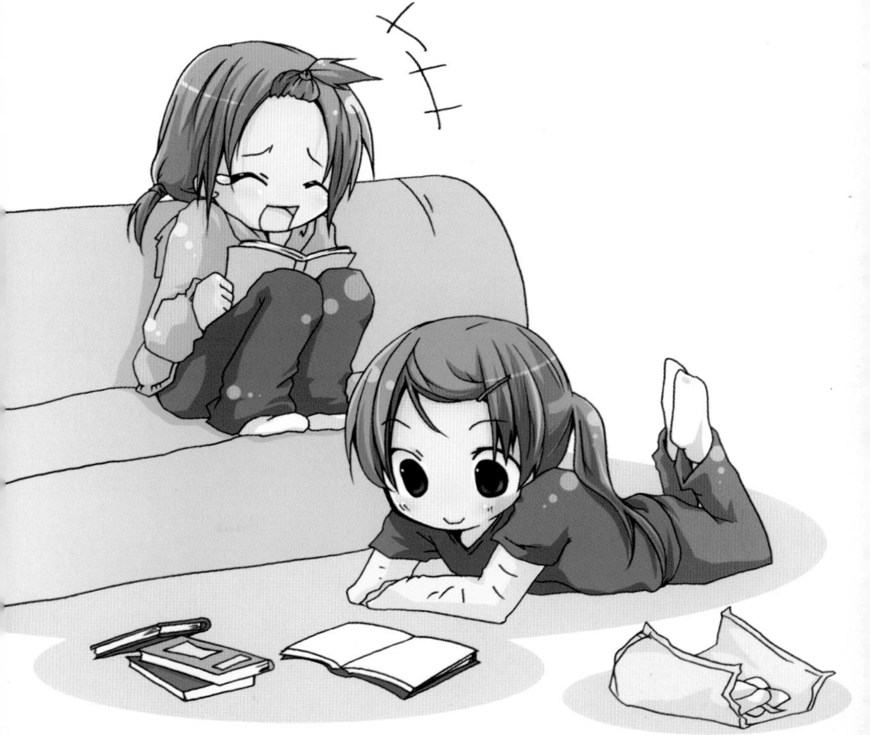

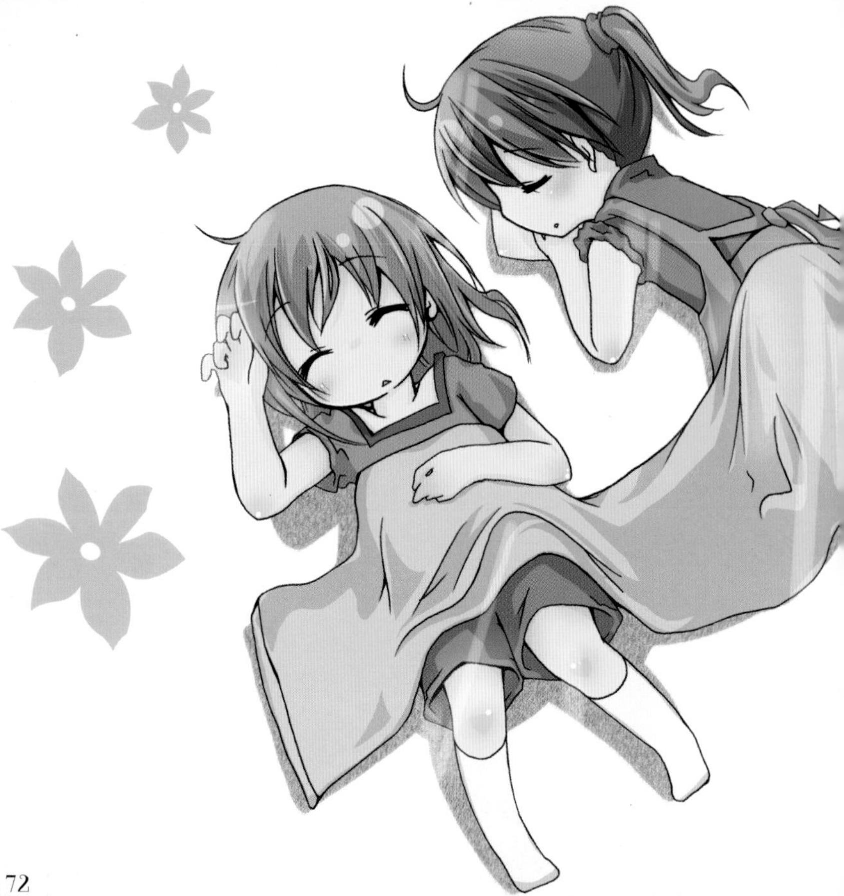

Afternoon naps
are twice as nice
when taken
with your sister.

午後の昼寝は姉と一緒だと、
倍も心地よい。

Sometimes
it's hard to watch
your big sister
grow up.

姉が成長してどんどん先へ行って
しまうのを見るのは、難しいこともある。

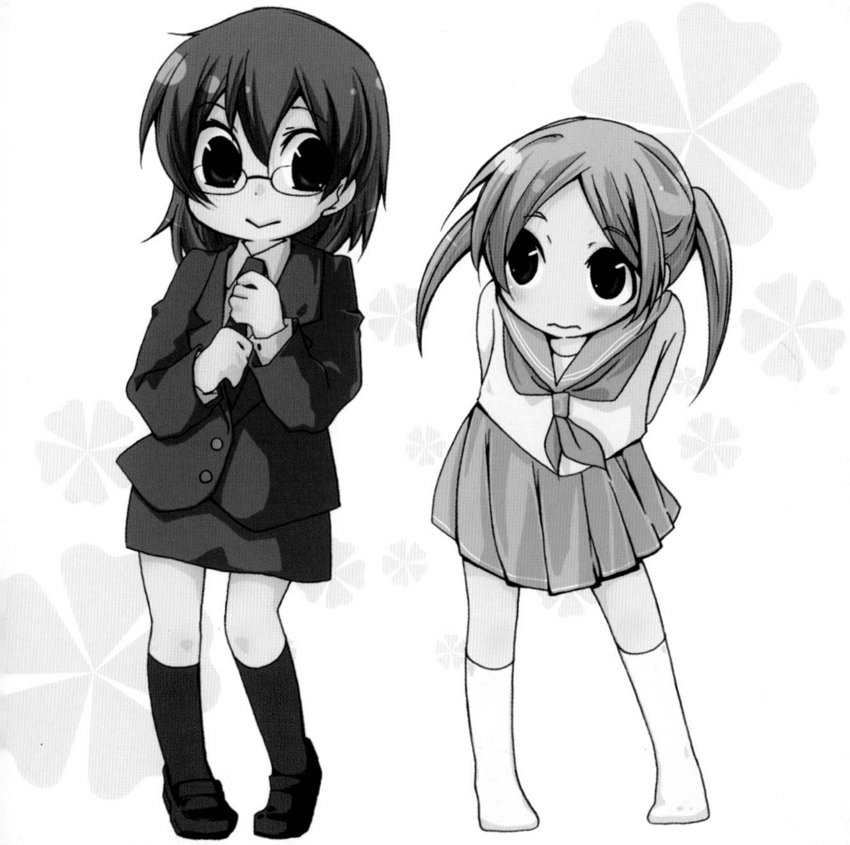

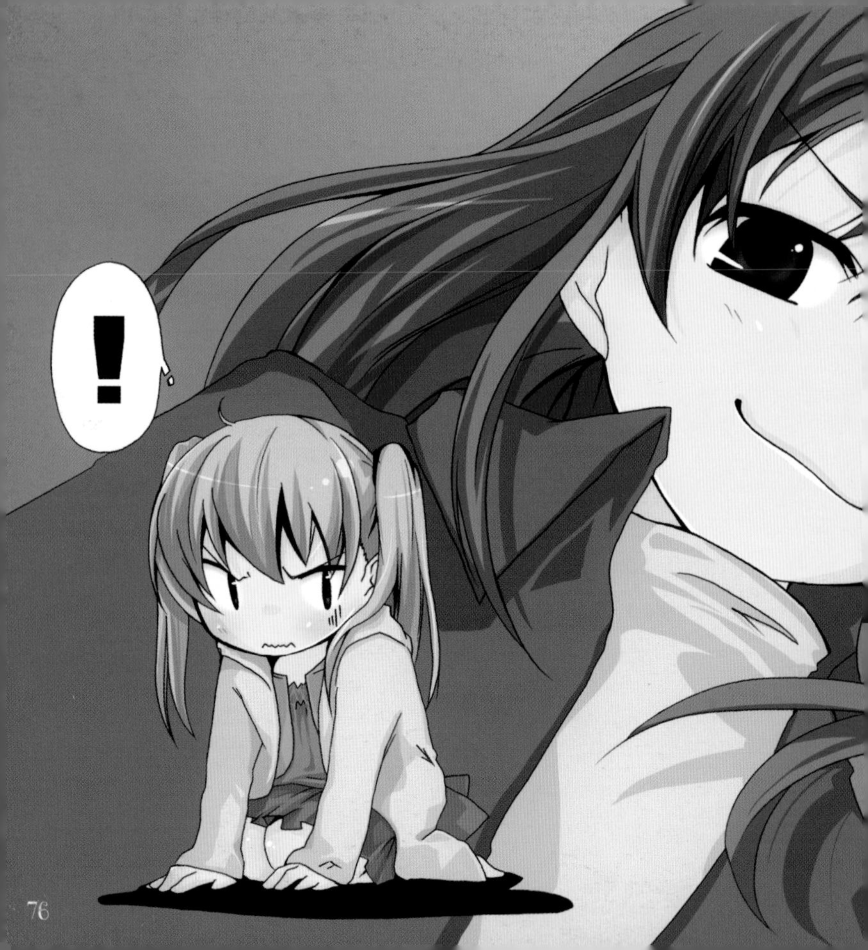
!

A sister's
shadow
can be hard
to escape.

姉の影から逃れるのは難しい。

It's not always easy
to follow in
your sister's footsteps...
but it's fun trying!

姉さんの後を追いかけていくのは簡単
ではないけれど、そうすることは楽しい！

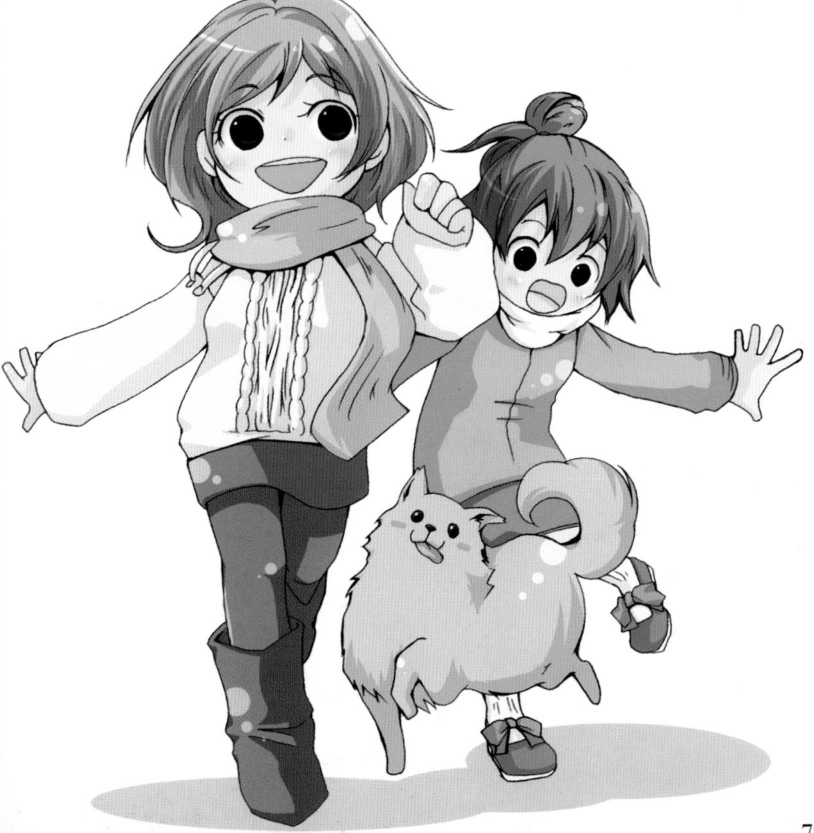

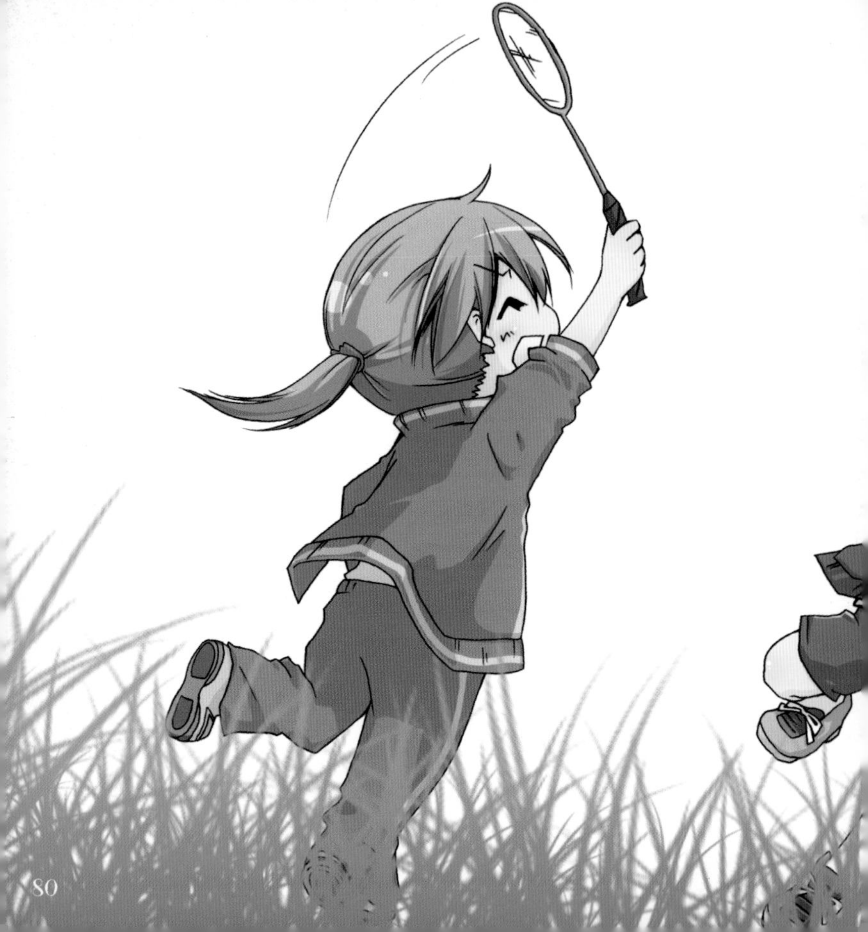

Letting your
sister win
is the
greatest
act of
kindness.

妹を勝たせてやるのは、
本当に優しいことだ。

Sisters warm
each other's hearts
even on
the coldest days.

一番寒い日にも、
姉妹はお互いの心を暖めあう。

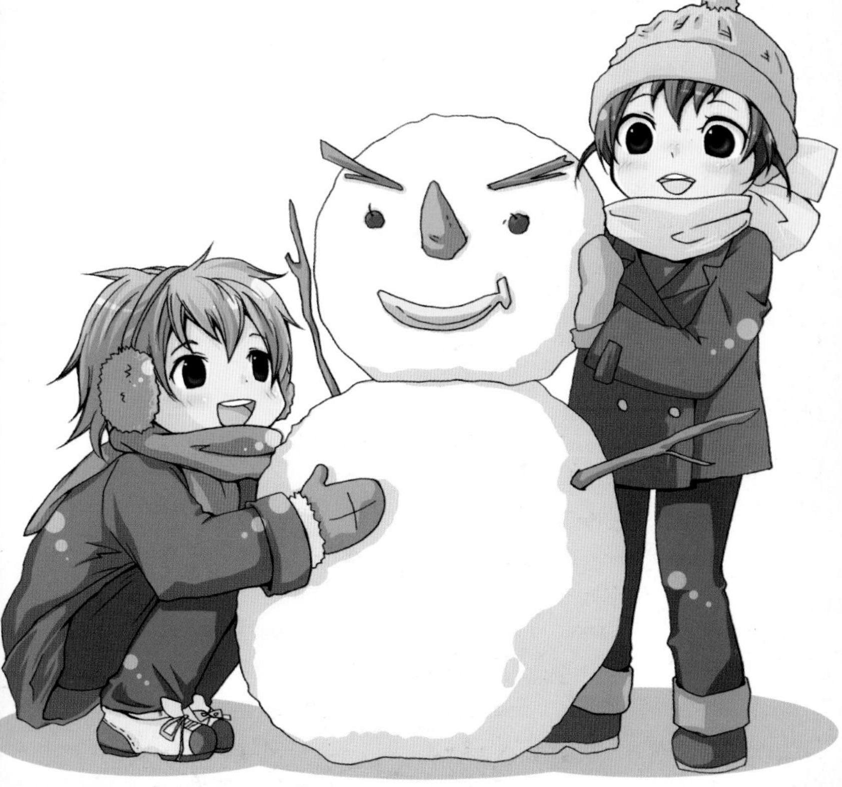

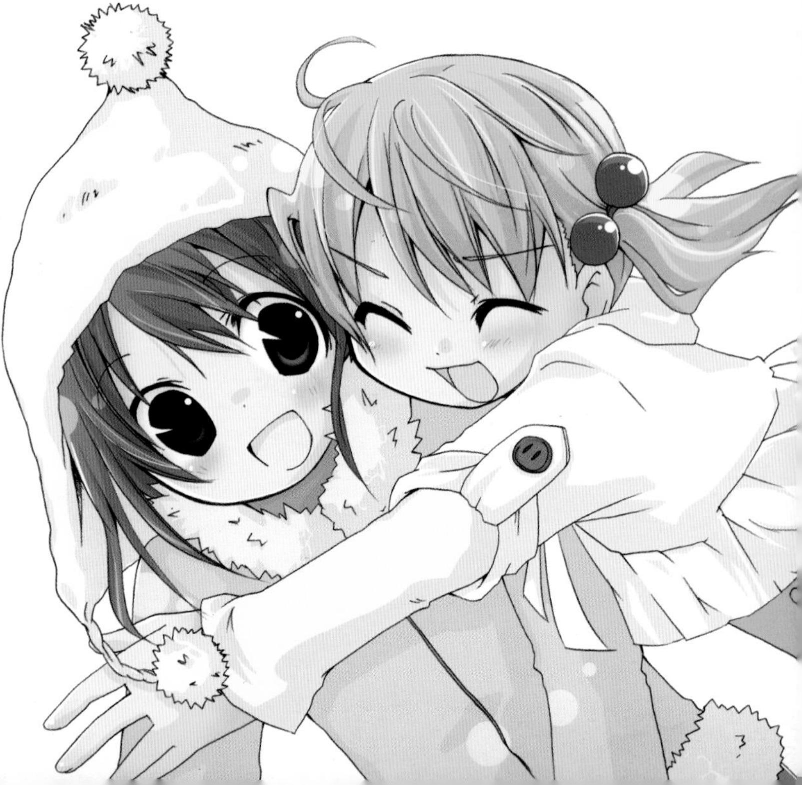

Little sisters give
the biggest hugs.

ぎゅっと一番強く
抱きしめてくれるのは、妹だ。

Reading and Writing

<ruby>日<rt>に</rt>本<rt>ほん</rt>語<rt>ご</rt></ruby>
(Japanese)

Japanese sentences are written using a combination of *hiragana*, which is used for phonetic spellings of Japanese words, as well as participles, prefixes and suffixes; *katakana*, for words of foreign origin; and *kanji*, the complex Chinese characters that represent the vast majority of words used in Japanese.

In addition, small hiragana (called *furigana*) are sometimes written above the kanji to assist readers who do not know the pronunciation of those characters.

The charts on the following pages show the 46 hiragana and katakana characters in their basic and modified forms, with pronunciations written in roman characters (*romaji*). The Japanese language has 5 vowels:

a as in ah · *i* as in we · *u* as in soon · *e* as in get · *o* as in old

Consonants are virtually the same as those heard in English except for the "f" sound, which is considerably softer in Japanese, and the "l" sound, which falls between a "d" and an "r" sound.

あ a	い i	う u	え e	お o
か ka	き ki	く ku	け ke	こ ko
さ sa	し shi	す su	せ se	そ so
た ta	ち chi	つ tsu	て te	と to
な na	に ni	ぬ nu	ね ne	の no
は ha	ひ hi	ふ fu	へ he	ほ ho
ま ma	み mi	む mu	め me	も mo
や ya		ゆ yu		よ yo
ら ra	り ri	る ru	れ re	ろ ro
わ wa				を o
				ん n

The 46 Basic Hiragana Characters
Each character represents one syllable.

ア a	イ i	ウ u	エ e	オ o
カ ka	キ ki	ク ku	ケ ke	コ ko
サ sa	シ shi	ス su	セ se	ソ so
タ ta	チ chi	ツ tsu	テ te	ト to
ナ na	ニ ni	ヌ nu	ネ ne	ノ no
ハ ha	ヒ hi	フ fu	ヘ he	ホ ho
マ ma	ミ mi	ム mu	メ me	モ mo
ヤ ya		ユ yu		ヨ yo
ラ ra	リ ri	ル ru	レ re	ロ ro
ワ wa				ヲ o
				ン n

The 46 Basic Katakana Characters
Each character represents one syllable.

Contracted Hiragana

A small や, ゆ or よ can be added to any hiragana character that ends in an "i" vowel (except for the character い itself) to form a contracted sound.

き や kya	き ゆ kyu	き よ kyo
し や sha	し ゆ shu	し よ sho
ち や cha	ち ゆ chu	ち よ cho
に や nya	に ゆ nyu	に よ nyo
ひ や hya	ひ ゆ hyu	ひ よ hyo
み や mya	み ゆ myu	み よ myo
り や rya	り ゆ ryu	り よ ryo
ぎ や gya	ぎ ゆ gyu	ぎ よ gyo
じ や ja	じ ゆ ju	じ よ jo
び や bya	び ゆ byu	び よ byo
ぴ や pya	ぴ ゆ pyu	ぴ よ pyo

キャ kya	キュ kyu	キョ kyo
シャ sha	シュ shu	ショ sho
チャ cha	チュ chu	チョ cho
ニャ nya	ニュ nyu	ニョ nyo
ヒャ hya	ヒュ hyu	ヒョ hyo
ミャ mya	ミュ myu	ミョ myo
リャ rya	リュ ryu	リョ ryo
ギャ gya	ギュ gyu	ギョ gyo
ジャ ja	ジュ ju	ジョ jo
ビャ bya	ビュ byu	ビョ byo
ピャ pya	ピュ pyu	ピョ pyo

Contracted Katakana

Likewise, a small ヤ, ユ or ヨ can be added to any katakana character that ends in an "i" vowel sound (other than the character イ itself).

Two-Dash and One-Circle Hiragana and Katakana

To modify the sounds of certain kana, the Japanese add two small dashes (called *dakuten*) or a tiny circle (called a *handakuten*) to the characters.

が ga	ぎ gi	ぐ gu	げ ge	ご go
ざ za	じ ji	ず zu	ぜ ze	ぞ zo
だ da	ぢ ji	づ zu	で de	ど do
ば ba	び bi	ぶ bu	べ be	ぼ bo
ぱ pa	ぴ pi	ぷ pu	ぺ pe	ぽ po

ガ ga	ギ gi	グ gu	ゲ ge	ゴ go
ザ za	ジ ji	ズ zu	ゼ ze	ゾ zo
ダ da	ヂ ji	ツ zu	デ de	ド do
バ ba	ビ bi	ブ bu	ベ be	ボ bo
パ pa	ピ pi	プ pu	ペ pe	ポ po

The Sisters

Saori Takarai (that's her on the right, holding the doll) is the big sister. Like most big sisters, she gets a bit bossy at times. Especially during meetings with her publisher.

Misato Takarai (she's the one on the left, with the cat) is Saori's little sister. But she's also the middle sister. Which means she's the one who usually gets blamed when Saori or Miho do something wrong.

Miho Takarai, as you've figured out by now, is the youngest sister. (We don't have a picture of her, but we've heard she sort of looks like that doll.) Miho didn't help draw this book, but she undoubtedly inspired those who did.

All three sisters grew up in Gunma Prefecture, about 60 miles northwest of Tokyo.

MANGA UNIVERSITY

Gift Books

TOKYO   SAN FRANCISCO

ORDERING INFORMATION

Visit our campus store:
www.mangauniversity.com

Send us an email:
info@mangauniversity.com

Call us toll-free in the USA:
1-877-BUY-MANGA (877-289-6264)